FASHION DRAWING FOR FUTURE FASHIC

Creative fashion illustration projects and practical drawing tutorials

by Irina V. Ivanova



For permission for additional use please contact
Permissions, Art Design Project, Inc.
www.artdesignproject.com/permissions.html

**ISBN-13: 978-1-953408-10-5**

Book Website
www.fashioncroquis.com/junior
Email: contact@artdesignproject.com

Printed in U.S.A

**professional fashion resources for future fashion designers**

IRINA V. IVANOVA

**Art Design Project, Inc**
publishing fashion drawing resources since
2007

Fashion Croquis junior

www.FashionCroquis.com/junior

Color pencils for project
FASHION DRAWING for Juniors
Portfolio development. Project 1
Multilayered ruffled skirt and sleeveless top (bustie
Steps 10-11
Step 10
TIP from Iva
Do not rush, and do not push too much on your pencil to keep your shading smooth
Try your pencils in different w
one, two layers, graduate co
or combinations of differe
Do not use too many co
project
If you have a few ve
keep notes to rem
exactly was you
project
Gallery of illustrations created based on only one fashion figure template
Illustration #1
Step 2
Step 1
Illustration #2
Step 2
Build your vocabulary
Technical drawings (flats) for project 2
Front shoulder yoke
Topstitching for jacket
Cropped jacket
Waist band
Back hip yoke
Slash pocket

Step 1
Step 2
Step 3
FASHION DRAWI
for Juniors
FASHION DRAWING for future fashion designers
creative fashion illustration projects & practical drawing tutorials
IRINA V. IVANOVA
Art Design Project, Inc
Step 3
Step 3
AWING for Juniors
Seam-to-seam pocket
uis.com/junior

# Content
# Fashion Drawing for Juniors

- How to use the book....... 6
- Figure drawing fashion template (croquis) for Volume #1 .....7
- Collection of sketches ............ 9
- Gallery of illustrations created based on only one fashion figure template............10-15
- How to trace template (croquis) ..............16-18
- Basic tools you need to start your fashion drawing projects ................19
- Basic coloring technique with color pencils.............20-23
- Portfolio development. Project 1. Multilayered ruffled skirt and sleeveless top (bustier) .........24-31
- Face rendering in details for Project 1 .........32
- Technical drawings (flats) for Project 1.........33
- Portfolio development. Project 1. Multilayered ruffled skirt and sleeveless top (bustier). All steps at a glance .....34-35

- Portfolio development. Project 2. Multilayered look with bag and boots.......36-42
- Face rendering in details for Project 2 ........ 43
- Color pencils for Project 2 .......44-45
- Build your vocabulary. Technical drawings (flats) for Project 2 ......46-47
- Portfolio development. Project 2. Multilayered look with bag and boots. All steps at a glance.....48-49
- Portfolio development. Project 3. Multilayered look with a long sweater, vest, and oversized scarf.....50-54
- Face rendering in details for Project 3.....55
- Build your vocabulary. Technical drawings (flats) for Project 3....56-57
- Portfolio development. Project 3. Multilayered look with a long sweater, vest, and oversized scarf. All steps at a glance.....58-59
- Portfolio development. Final result.....60
- What do you need to know about a portfolio?......63
- Hair drawing.....62-77
- About the author.......78

# How to use the book

Hello! My name is Iva. Follow me from page to page and enjoy the creative process of learning!

1

- Start your professional fashion design portfolio
- For this book, you will need basic art supplies (see page 19)

2

- Get inspired!
- Check out how much you can create with only one fashion drawing template (croquis) (see page 7)

3

Learn how to copy the template (see pages 16-17)

4

- Follow the step by step process and learn how you can start and finish three different projects (see pages 24-60)

5

- Learn how you can improve your skills in hair rendering (see pages 62-77)
- Check out beautiful imagery from Rijksmuseum, Amsterdam (see pages 72-77)
- Do your research and try to find more images for your inspiration for hair or garment design

6

- Keep practicing
- Do more sketches in different styles
- Enjoy the process
- Do not worry about your mistakes
- Embrace your mistake
- It is a learning process

7

- Collect the best projects in your portfolio

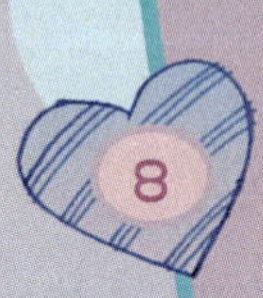

8

Check on the next edition of the book for more projects, templates, and new techniques

**Figure drawing fashion template (croquis) for Volume #1**

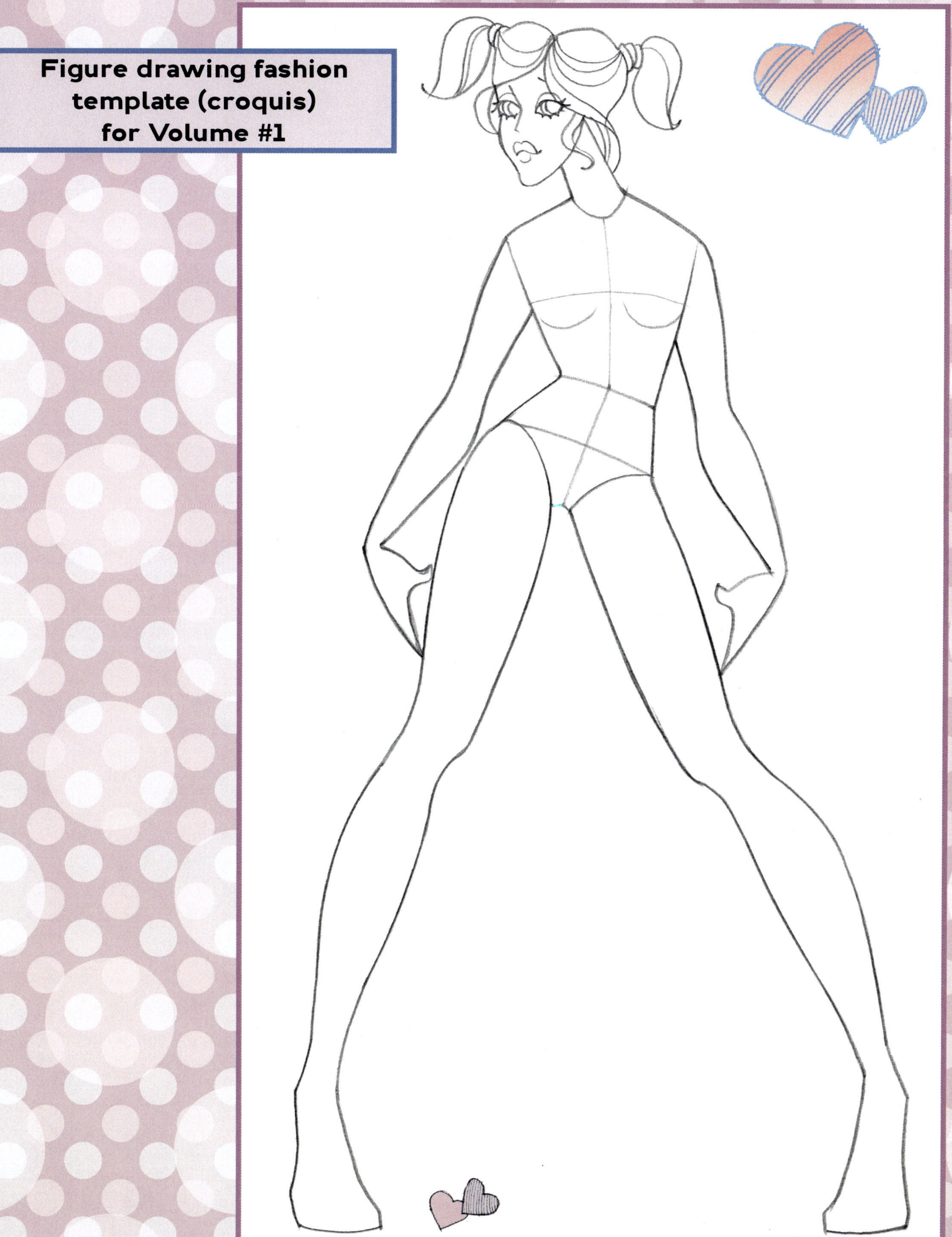

## Collection of sketches

# Gallery of illustrations created based on only one fashion figure template

See the fashion drawing template for all these illustrations on page 7

Step 1
Illustration #2
Step 2
Step 3
Illustration #3
Step 3
Step 1
Step 2

Illustration #4
Step 1
Step 2
Step 3
Illustration #5
Step 1
Step 2
Step 3

Illustration #6
Step 1
Step 2
Step 3
Illustration #7
Step 1
Step 2
Step 3

Step 1
Illustration #8
Step 2
Step 3
Illustration #9
Step 1
Step 2
Step 3

Illustration #10
Step 1
Step 2
Step 3
Illustration #11
Step 1
Step 2
Step 3

# How to trace template (croquis)

Step 1

Cover selected template with a sheet of see-through paper

See-through sheet of paper

Step 2

Trace selected figure drawing template using a simple pencil

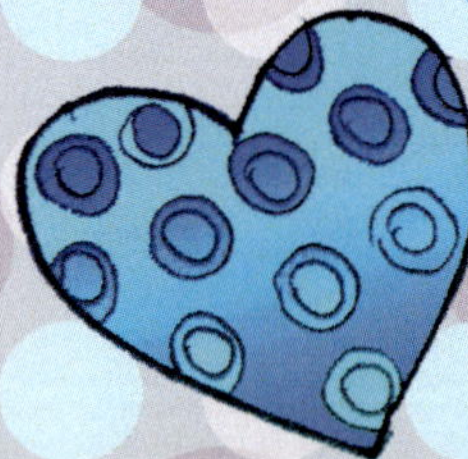

Croquis to be copied

Light copy pad

If your paper is not see-through, you can use a tracing light copy pad or box

- You got a copy of your template!
- Now you are ready to start sketching

- Start sketching your garment design
- Do not use very dark and heavy pencil lines
- Clean your sketch from unnecessary pencil lines, marks, corrections before coloring
- If your sketch is still not clean enough, copy your simple pencil drawing again to make sure your coloring will not be smudged with excessive simple pencil lines underneath

- It is time to color skin
- Choose any skin tone you like for the face and arms
- Start slow and light
- Later you can always add more color

Step 6

Start coloring from the lightest colors and finish with the darkest

Step 8

- Complete coloring
- If you do not like the final result, start from step 1 again

Step 7

Sign your final project and put it in your portfolio or frame it and give it as a present to somebody

## TIP from Iva

In this book (see pages 24-59), you will find three beautiful fashion illustration projects with very detailed instructions and easy to follow steps with color pencil rendering

## Build your vocabulary

A portfolio is a folder with see-through pages to collect your best artworks

# Basic tools you need to start your fashion drawing projects

Variety of erasers

## TIP from Iva

If you need an eraser with a sharp point for small details to erase, cut an eraser with scissors to create a such point

Mechanical, graphite simple pencils and pencil sharpener

French curves for drawing curved lines

- French curves are not mandatory tools
- You will need them only if you want to have perfect curve lines in your drawing
- Choose any size or form of French curve template and use it if you wish

- Use any simple pencil and eraser you have
- Just do not push too much on your pencil yet
- Keep your line light and easy to correct if necessary

Variety of color pencils

- Color pencils are essential!
- Choose any good quality color pencils. Just make sure they are soft or smooth for easy coloring and blending
- Maybe it will be a good idea to buy only a few color pencils of your favorite colors to start
- After you try different color pencils, you will understand which brand is best for you

# Basic coloring technique with color pencils

## Two different methods to hold a pencil

Holding pencil close to the lid

1

- To draw a sharp line, hold a pencil close to the lid
- Use this holding method for small details or final outlining

Holding pencil far away from the lid

2

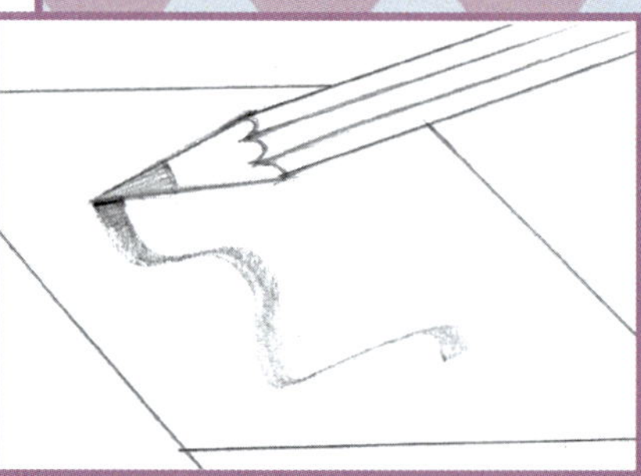

- To draw a smooth and soft line, do not hold a pencil close to the lid
- Use this holding method for coloring big drawing area

TIP from Iva

Practice coloring before you start a project

**Build your vocabulary**

Rendering is a synonym for coloring

## *Color pencils rendering practice*

- Use method #2 to hold the pencil
- Move slow and in the same horizontal direction
- Do not push too much on the pencil
- Try to keep uniform coloring

- Use method #2 to hold the pencil
- Use one color pencil
- Move slow and in the same horizontal direction
- Do not push too much on the pencil
- Try to color from light to dark with soft blending in between

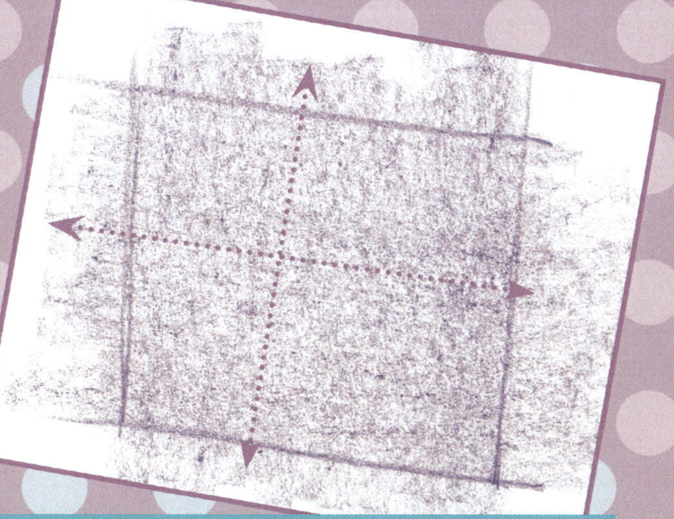

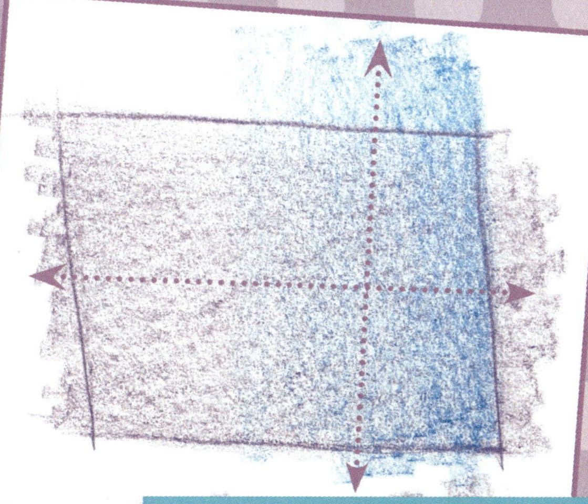

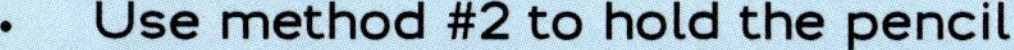

- Use method #2 to hold the pencil
- Move slow and in the same horizontal direction
- After that, do the same coloring in a vertical direction
- Do not push too much on the pencil
- This method is the best to darken your coloring
- Use as many layers of rendering as you need

- Use method #2 to hold the pencils
- Use two different color pencils
- Move slow and in the same horizontal direction with one pencil
- Change the color pencil and direction of coloring
- Try to color from one color to another with soft blending in between

## *Choose the right color pencil for skin rendering*

- You need any smooth or soft good quality color pencils
- Try different color pencils for skin rendering
- Write down the name or numbers of each pencil for future references

- Pay attention to the overlapping of different colors
- Maybe the overlapping of different colors will give you your best skin tone

Overlapping of two different skin tone colors

One layer of skin tone color

## Choose the right drawing paper

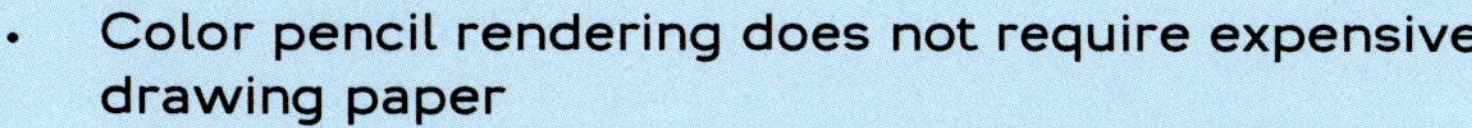

- Color pencil rendering does not require expensive drawing paper
- Any drawing paper for dry media will be OK
- Try different drawing paper brands
- The texture of your skin rendering will depend on the surface of your drawing paper
- Cold press drawing paper has a more textured surface than hot press drawing paper
- If face rendering is essential for you, choose hot press drawing paper
- It is easier to keep smooth skin coloring with lighter color pencils and a smooth surface of drawing paper

Cold press drawing paper (very textured coloring)

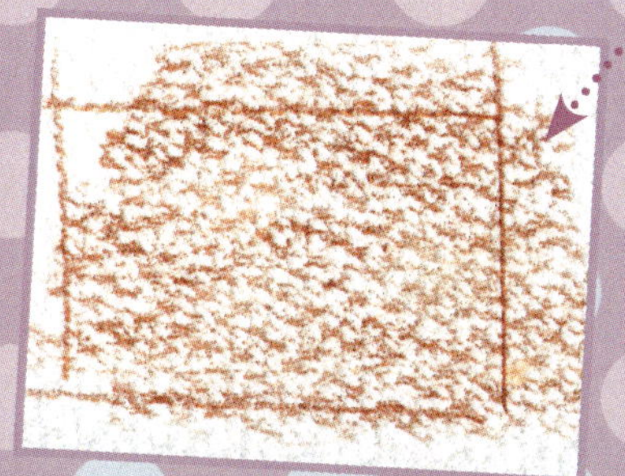

Cold press drawing paper (textured coloring, but it is not so visible because of the light color)

Hot press drawing paper (smooth coloring)

### TIP from Iva

Skin coloring in fashion illustration is not mandatory, so you can skip this part altogether and focus only on the garment rendering

# Portfolio development. Project 1

## Multilayered ruffled skirt and sleeveless top (bustier)

## Steps 1-3

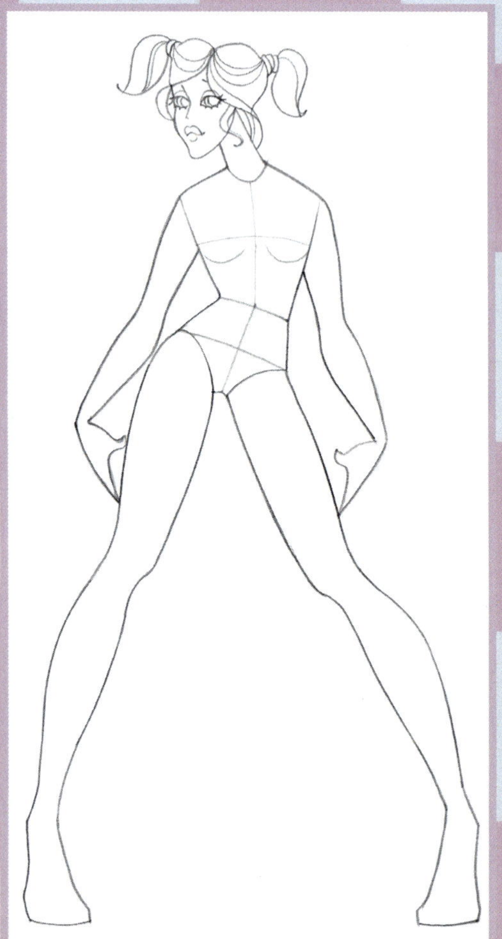

Step 1

TIP from Iva

More templates are in Fashion Sketchbook ISBN 9781953408099

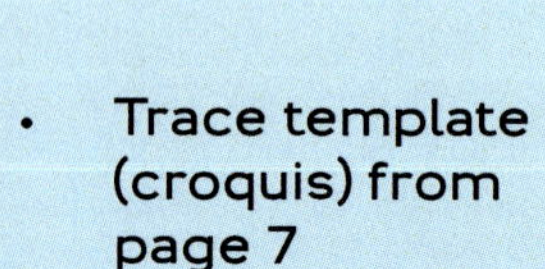

- Trace template (croquis) from page 7
- Keep your tracing line very light because you will need to do some corrections later

- Outline basic shape for a garment
- Keep your line loose
- Do not be afraid to make mistakes because you always have an eraser
- Try to catch the "mood" of your future design, do not worry about details yet

- Now is time to think about details
- Show ruffles on skirt and shoes
- Make darker outlining for face, arms, and legs

## Build your vocabulary

The ruffles are extra pieces of gathered or pleated fabric used for garment decoration

# Portfolio development. Project 1
## Multilayered ruffled skirt and sleeveless top (bustier)
## Steps 4-5

### Build your vocabulary

The neckline is a line around and closest to the neck

A bustier is a top closely fitted to the body. Historically originated from underwear

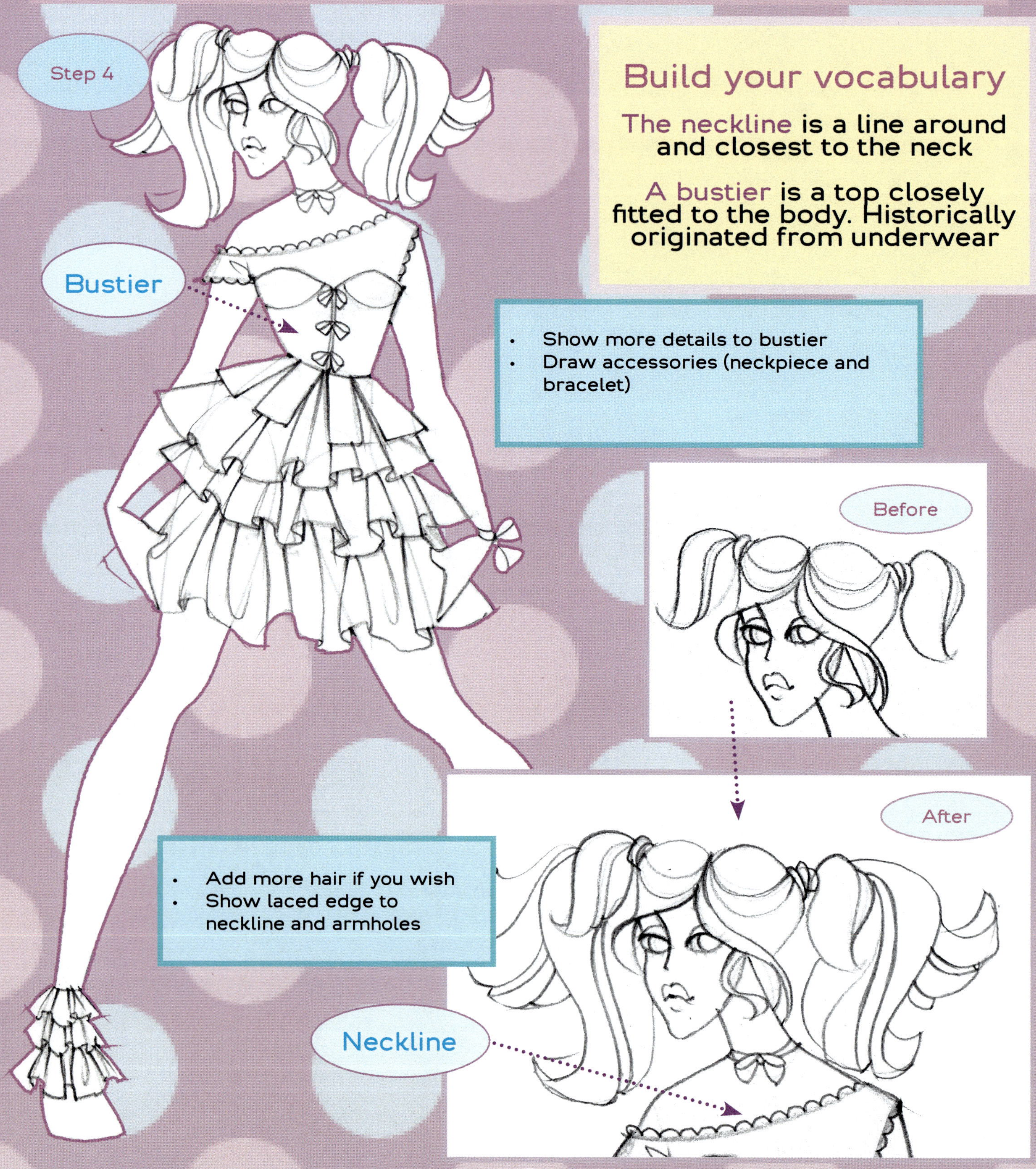


- Show more details to bustier
- Draw accessories (neckpiece and bracelet)

- Add more hair if you wish
- Show laced edge to neckline and armholes

- Now is time to think about more details
- Outline and do light shading for eyes
- Draw a binding line for all edges of the bustier and peplum

## Build your vocabulary

Peplum is an additional small part of the garment connected with the waistline

A binding is a narrow strip of fabric (could be in contrast colors) used to secure or clean finish the raw edges of a garment

# Portfolio development. Project 1
## Multilayered ruffled skirt and sleeveless top (bustier)
## Steps 6-9

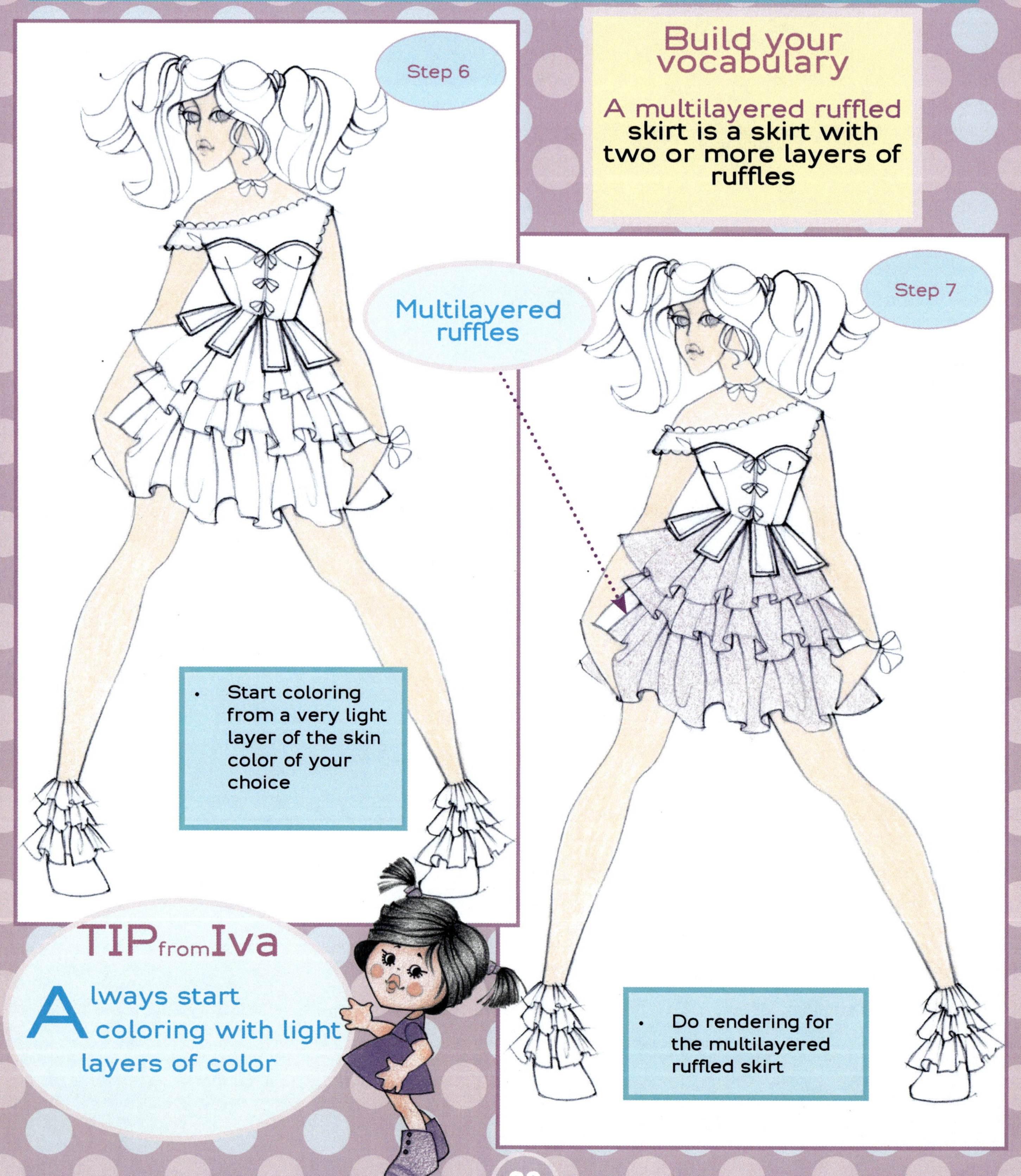

## TIP from Iva

To avoid smudging, always keep under your drawing hand a clean sheet of paper

- Chose a color for hair
- Do the first layer of hair rendering
- Start rendering for small details like accessories (neckpiece and bracelet) and shoes

- Do rendering for bustier

- For the second layer of hair coloring, use the same pencil you used for the first layer of hair coloring, but push a little harder on the pencil

# Portfolio development. Project 1
## Multilayered ruffled skirt and sleeveless top (bustier)
## Steps 10-11

TIP from Iva

Do not rush, and do not push too much on your pencil to keep your shading smooth

- With the same color pencils, go to the second layer of rendering to show shading for the skirt and hair
- Add more color to the face (lips and eyes)
- Start second rendering for small details like accessories and shoes

Step 11
TIP from Iva
For final outlining, always use a very sharp pencil and sharpen it as often as needed
• Do final outlining for some details to complete your project
• Make sure your pencil for outlining is very sharp

# Face rendering in details for project 1

- Just first layer of skin rendering

- The first layer of rendering for hair
- Add more color to the face (lips and eyes)
- Add more dark rendering (like you use for lips) for upper eyelids

After

- Add more color for chicks and neck under the face
- Add shadows for hair
- Outline with a dark or black pencil some details to complete the illustration

## Color pencils for project 1

- Light Peach color pencil - for skin rendering
- Yellow Ochre color pencil - for hair and fitted top
- Violet color pencil - for skirt and accessories
- Cobalt Blue color pencil - for eyes
- Black color pencil - for outlining

## Technical drawings (flats) for project 1

Bustier with peplum

Fitted blouse

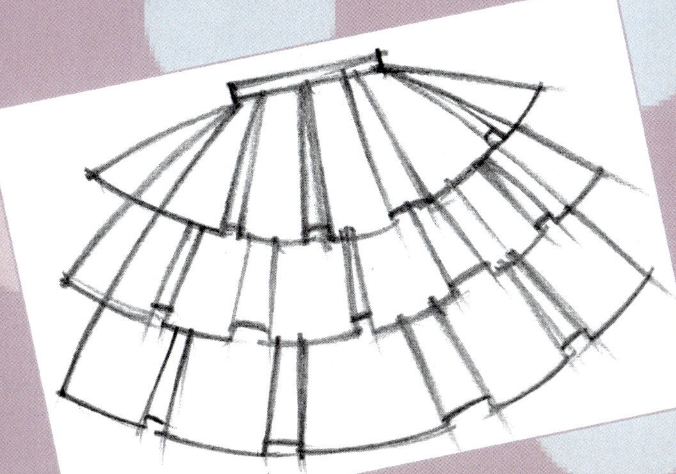

Multilayered ruffled skirt

# Portfolio development. Project 1
## Multilayered ruffled skirt and sleeveless top (bustier)
## All steps at a glance

7
8
9
10
11
Congratulation! You have completed project #1

# Portfolio development. Project 2
## Multilayered look with bag and boots
## Steps 1-3

- Trace template (croquis) from page 7
- Keep your tracing line very light because you will need to do some corrections later

- Outline basic shape for a cropped jacket, boots, and shoulder bag
- Keep your line loose
- Place a few lines in the elbows and ankles areas for future wrinkled details

**TIP from Iva**

More templates are in Fashion Sketchbook
ISBN 9781953408099

- Make darker outlining for face, hair, hands
- Draw fitted pants with a few wrinkles in the knee area
- Complete outlining wrinkled socks

## Build your vocabulary

A messenger bag is a bag with a long crossbody strap

# Portfolio development. Project 2
## Multilayered look with bag and boots
## Steps 4-5

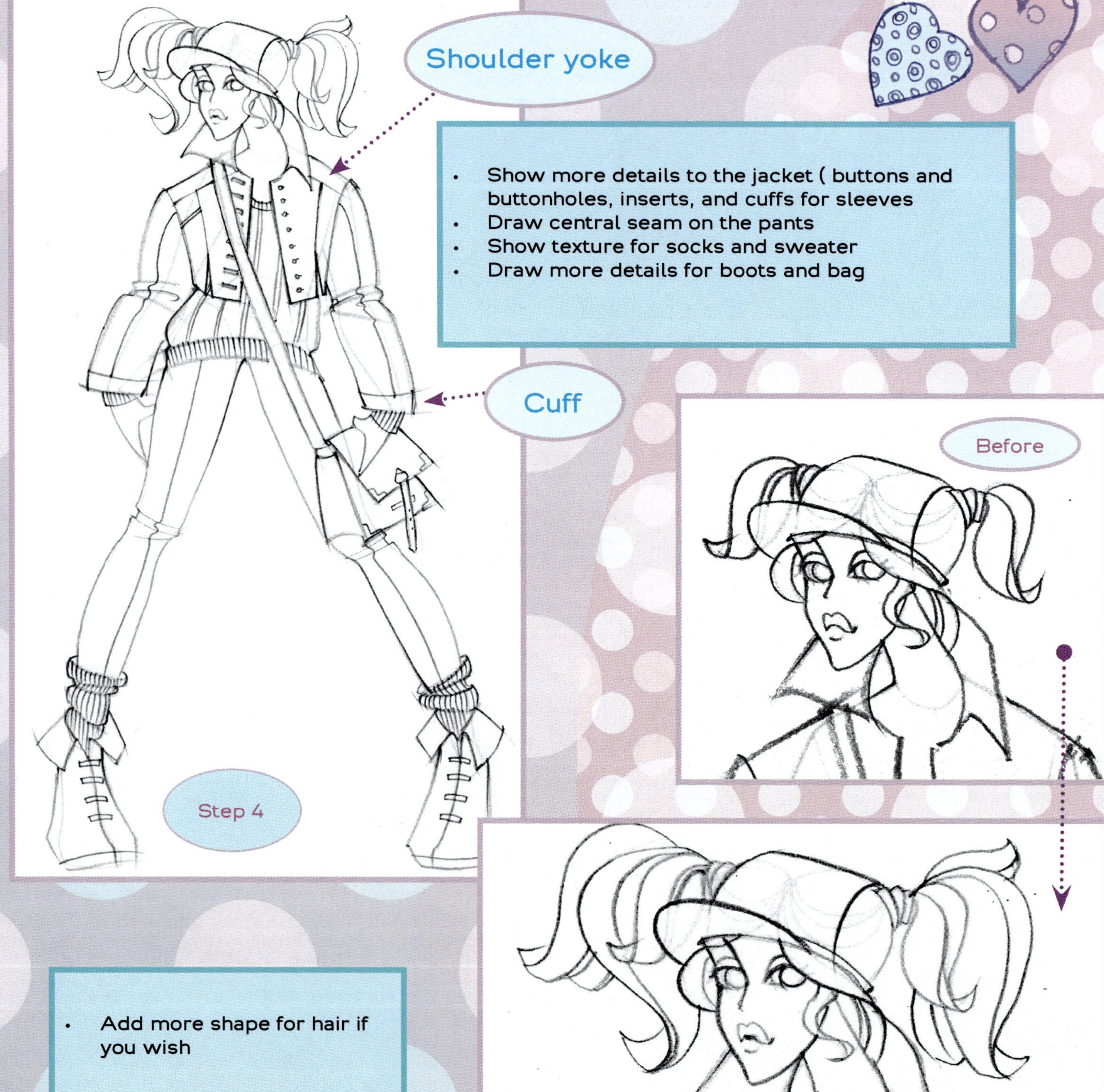


- Show more details to the jacket ( buttons and buttonholes, inserts, and cuffs for sleeves
- Draw central seam on the pants
- Show texture for socks and sweater
- Draw more details for boots and bag

- Add more shape for hair if you wish

Step 5
- Now is time to think about sewing details (topstitching for jacket, pants, and hat
Topstitching for sleeves
Before
- Show texture for turndown boots
Topstitching for pants
After
Faux fur turndown
TIP from Iva
Do not rush then draw details
Leather inserts

# Portfolio development. Project 2
## Multilayered look with bag and boots
## Steps 6-10

- Start with very light first layers of rendering for skin (step 6), cropped jacket (step 7), and fitted pants (step 8)

- Start rendering for small details like accessories (shoes and hat)

- Chose a color for hair
- Do the first layer of hair rendering

TIP from Iva

To avoid smudging, always keep under your drawing hand a clean sheet of paper

# Portfolio development. Project 2
## Multilayered look with bag and boots
## Step 11

- Do final outlining for some details to complete your project
- Make sure your pencil for outlining is very sharp

**TIP from Iva**

Do not rush, and do not push too much on your pencil to keep your shading smooth

- With the same color pencils, go to the second rendering layer to show shading for the jacket, pants, and hair
- Add more color to the face (lips and eyes)
- Start second rendering for small details like a messenger bag, hat, and shoes

# Face rendering in details for project 2

## TIP from Iva

For final outlining, always use a very sharp pencil and sharpen it as often as needed

# Color pencils for project 2

- Try your pencils in different ways: one, two layers, graduate coloring, or combinations of different colors
- Do not use too many colors in one project
- If you have a few very similar colors, keep notes to remember which one exactly was your final choice for the project

Color pencils for skin rendering
Pink Rose (one layer)
Pink Rose (two layers)
Pink Rose (one layer)
Light Peach (one layer)
Light Peach and Pink Rose (overlapping)
Color pencil for eyes rendering
Cobalt Blue
Color pencil for hair and pants rendering
Yellow Ochre
Color pencil for jacket,shoes, hat and bag rendering
Violet
Do not forget about basic black pencil for final detailing

# Build your vocabulary
## Technical drawings (flats) for project 2

## Fitted pants

### TIP from Iva
### Build your vocabulary

Try to remember basic garment terminology and learn how professionally to describe your bright design idea

# Portfolio development. Project 2
## Multilayered look with bag and boots
## All steps at a glance

7
8
9
10
11

# Portfolio development. Project 3

## Multilayered look with a long sweater, vest, and oversized scarf

## Steps 1–3

- Trace template (croquis) from page 7
- Keep your tracing line very light because you will need to do some correction with croquis later

- Outline basic shape for a vest, sweater, boots, hat, and scarf
- Keep your line loose
- Place a few lines in the elbow, waistline, knee, and wrist areas for future wrinkled details



TIP from Iva

More templates are in Fashion Sketchbook ISBN 9781953408099

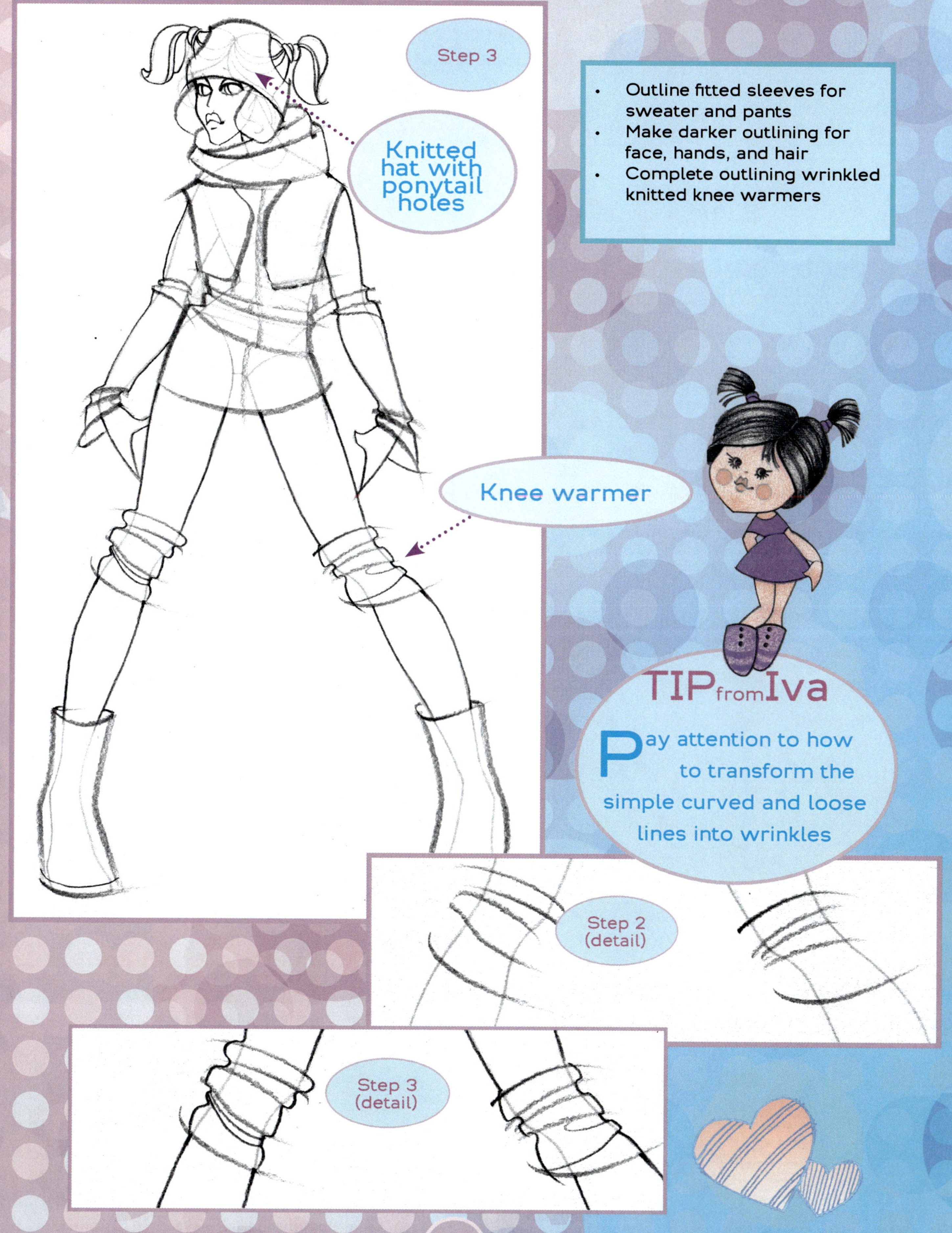


- Outline fitted sleeves for sweater and pants
- Make darker outlining for face, hands, and hair
- Complete outlining wrinkled knitted knee warmers

TIP from Iva

Pay attention to how to transform the simple curved and loose lines into wrinkles

# Portfolio development. Project 3

## Multilayered look with a long sweater, vest, and oversized scarf

## Steps 4-8

- Draw binding for hat and vest
- Show texture for wrinkled knitted knee warmers
- Draw long fringe for the scarf

- Erase all unnecessary line
- Add more details
- Be ready for coloring

Step 6

Binding

- Start with very light first layers of rendering for skin (step 6), fitted pants (step 7), hair, and vest (step 8)

Step 8

## Build your vocabulary

Fringe is a decorative border or edge for garment and accessories

# Portfolio development. Project 3

## Multilayered look with a long sweater, vest, and oversized scarf

## Step 9

Step 9

- Now is time to think about details
- Color binding for hat and vest
- Complete rendering for scarf fringe and stripes
- Draw details on boots

# Face rendering in details for project 3

- Just first layer of skin rendering

- The first layer of rendering for hair
- Add more color to the face (lips and eyes)
- Add more dark rendering (like you use for lips) for upper eyelids

- Add the second layer or rendering for the face to smooth out the texture of the paper
- Add shadows for hair
- Outline with a dark or black pencil some details to complete the illustration

To smooth out face texture, use a darker skin tone pencil for the first layer and a lighter skin ton pencil for the second layer of the face rendering

# Build your vocabulary
## Technical drawings (flats) for project 3

TIP from Iva
Build your vocabulary

Practice describing any of your favorite garments to improve your professional language

Color pencils for project 3

- Terra Cotta and Nectar color pencils - for skin rendering
- Yellow Ochre color pencil - for the vest
- Violet color pencil - for pants and accessories
- Black color pencil - for hair and final outlining

# Portfolio development. Project 3
## Multilayered look with a long sweater, vest, and oversized scarf
## All steps at a glance

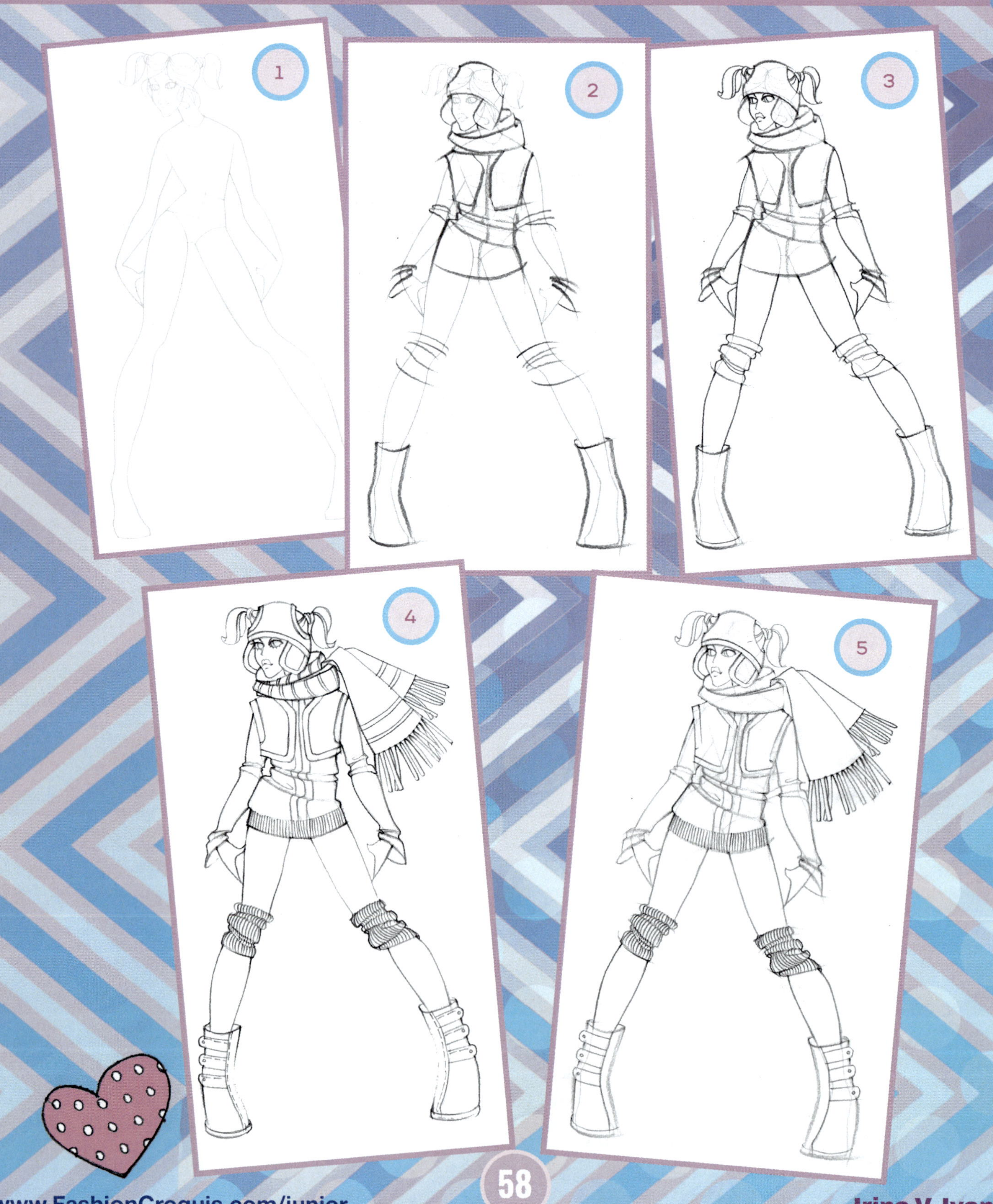

6
7
8
9

# Portfolio development
# Final result

*One template (croquis) and three different outcomes*

## What do you need to know about a portfolio?

- A portfolio is a professional way to show your best projects to somebody
- A portfolio is a tool to keep your best drawings very neat and clean
- A portfolio will help you to be organized
- A portfolio will help you to see all your best projects at a glance
- You may have a few different portfolios for diverse collections of illustrations (party dresses portfolio, casual garment portfolio of costume illustrations for favorite movies)
- A portfolio will keep you motivated
- Keep your existing portfolio always up-to-date with new best illustrations
- Keep practicing, enjoy the process, always try to do your best
- A portfolio is always a work in progress

# Hair drawing

## Hair line

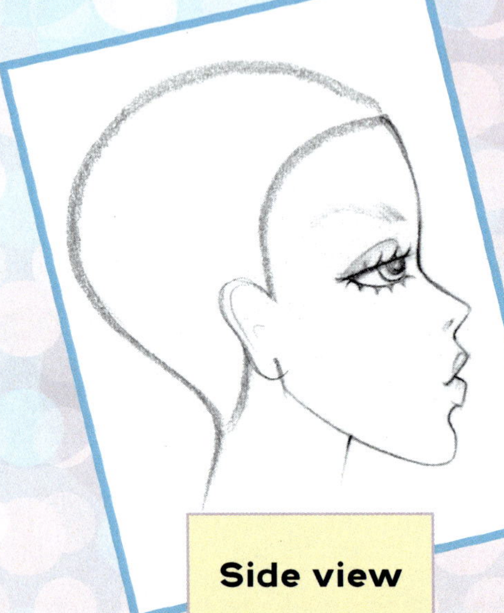

Side view

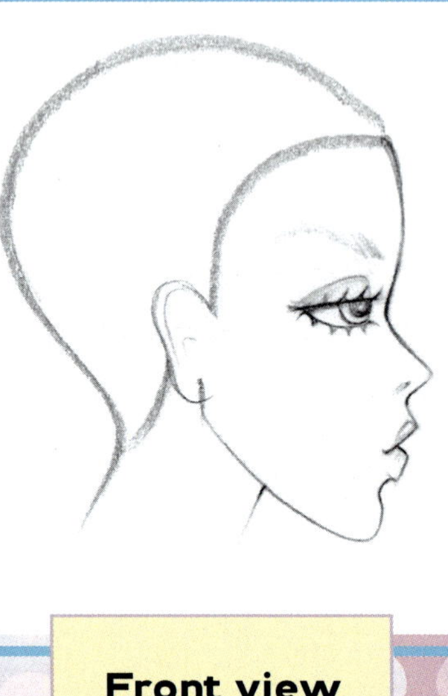

Front view

3/4 view

## Hair with bang

Outlining of hair shape

Outlining of head

Step 1

### TIP from Iva

Start to draw hair as one big shape and only after that give the directions and a few lines to show individual strands

- To give volume to hair, keep shape for hair always more prominent than the shape of the head
- Do not draw any details before you choose an overall shape for a hairdo

Step 2

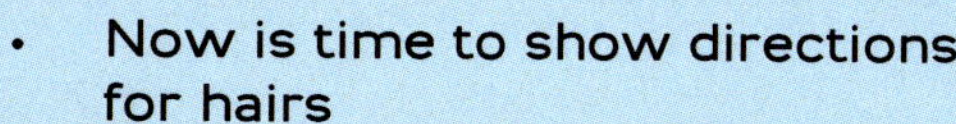

- Now is time to show directions for hairs
- Do not draw directional lines too straight and follow the shape of the head

Step 3

- Do any corrections if needed for directional hairlines and hair shape

Darker lines

Lighter lines

Darker lines

"Openings" in hair shape

Step 4

- Do final rendering
- Show a few "openings" in hair shape
- To emphasize smoothness of hair, do darker hair outlining in the end and at the beginning of hairs

## Hair with side part

## Ponytail

Short hair
(side view)
Step 1
Step 2
Step 3
Short hair
(3/4 view)
Step 1
Step 2
Step 3

Are you ready for a challenge?

# Keep one hairstyle and try three different hair length

- Outline the basic hair shape

Ear length

Chin length

Shoulder length

• Show direction of hair flowing
• Pay attention to details

Are you ready for a challenge?

# Let's learn how to draw curly hair

Example #1

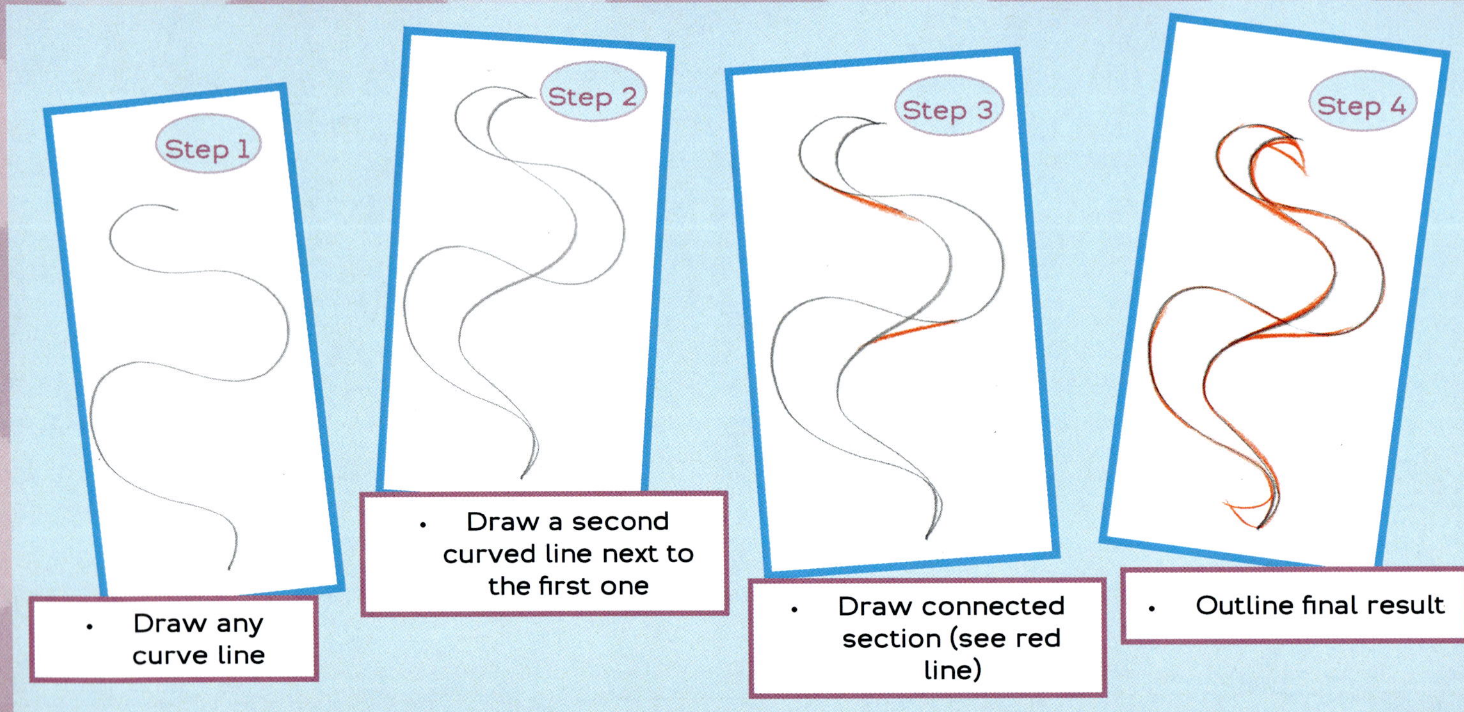


Example #2

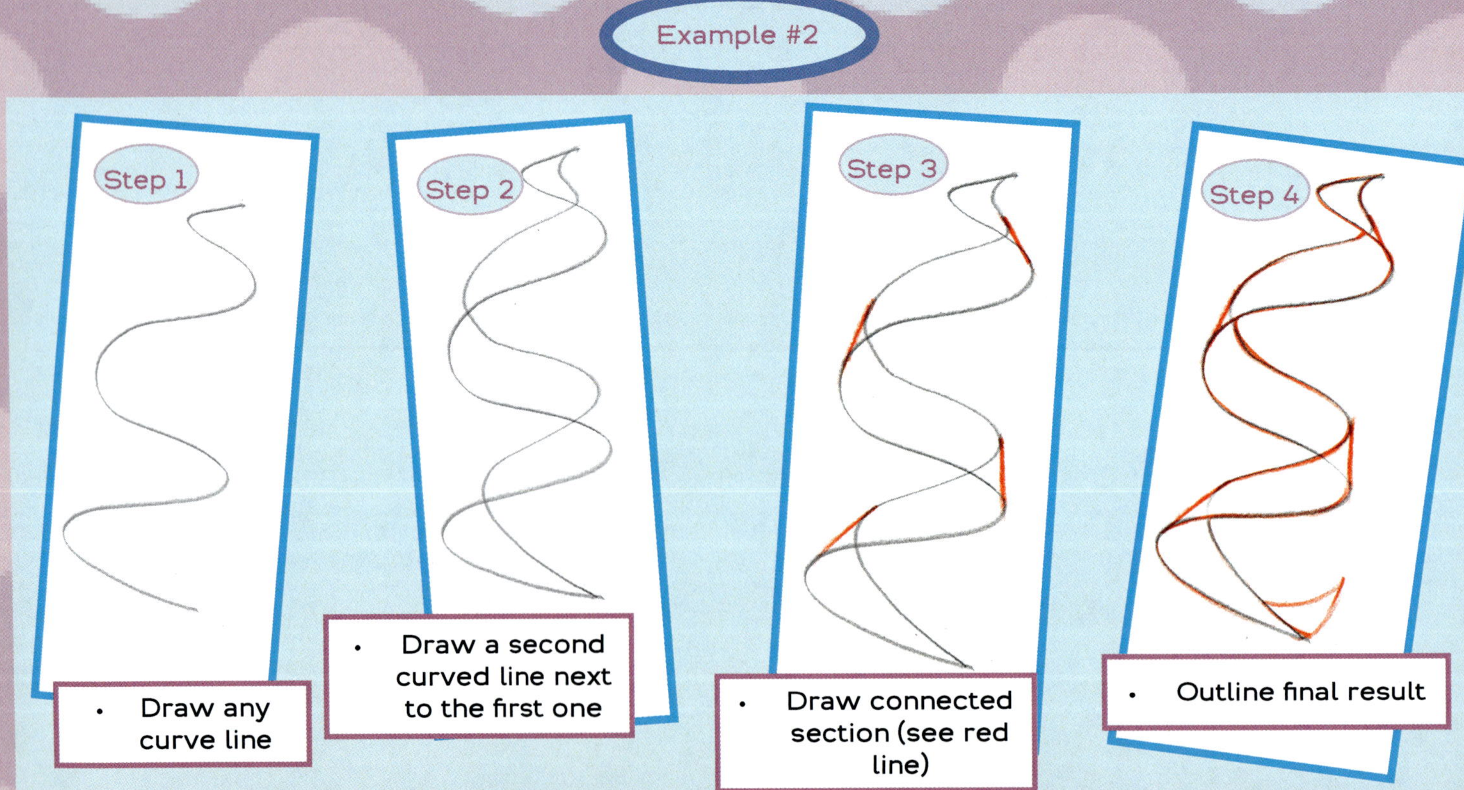

# Side ponytail

# Let's learn how to draw braid

Are you ready for a challenge?

Example #1

Example #2

## Braid (side view)

## Braid ending

# More hairstyles for your inspiration

Are you ready to create your hairstyle?

Style 1

Style 2

Style 3

Coëffure à l'Euridice

Image source (Rijksmuseum, Amsterdam)

Image source (Rijksmuseum, Amsterdam)

Image source
(Rijksmuseum, Amsterdam)
Style 4
Style 5
Style 6
Image source
(Rijksmuseum, Amsterdam)

# More hairstyles for your inspiration

Image source (Rijksmuseum, Amsterdam)

Image source (Rijksmuseum, Amsterdam)

Image source (Rijksmuseum, Amsterdam)

Image source (Rijksmuseum, Amsterdam)

# More hairstyles for your inspiration

Style 14

Style 15

Style 16

Image source
(Rijksmuseum, Amsterdam)

COËFFURE AUX CHARMES DE LA LIBERTÉ
Se trouve à Paris Chez Depain Cœffeur de Dames, et Auteur de cette Cœffure.
Rue St. Honoré au coin de celle d'Orléans, au 1.er au-dessus du Caffé, au Grand Balcon.
AVEC PRIVILEGE DU ROI
Nb. Le Sr. Depain continue toujours d'enseigner l'Art de Cœffer.

Image source
(Rijksmuseum, Amsterdam)

Image source
(Rijksmuseum, Amsterdam)
Style 17
Style 18
Style 19
Image source
(Rijksmuseum, Amsterdam)

# About the author

Irina V. Ivanova is the author of Fashion Croquis books and sketchbooks.

As an experienced educator, professional fashion designer, and trained illustrator Irina delights in merging her versatile professional experiences in a blend of fashion, art, and educational resources.

As a fashion illustrator, Irina combines her profound knowledge of clothing design with artistry.

In her fashion drawing books, Irina balances the creative and technical aspects of the clothing design process.

In addition to her Fashion Design publishing projects, as a professional illustrator, Irina creates coloring books, journals, and wall art.

Irina creates her books and art projects in her Florida-based studio.

## FASHION ACTIVITY BOOKS BY IRINA V. IVANOVA

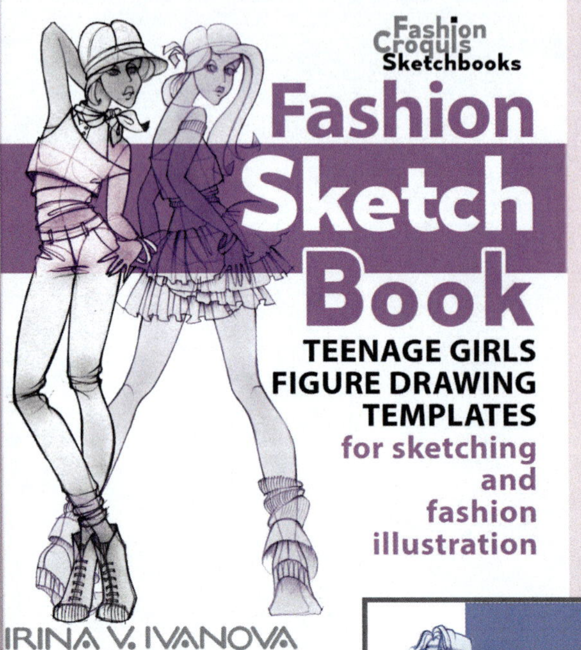


ISBN: 978-1953408099

**Fashion sketchbook:** Teenage girls figure drawing templates for sketching and fashion illustration

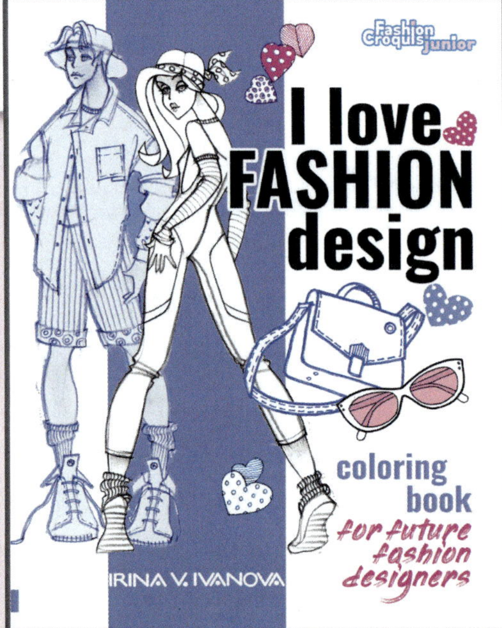


ISBN: 978-1953408112

**Fashion Coloring book:** Teenage fashion,clothing design and fashion accessories

ISBN:978-1953408136

ISBN: 978-1953408129

## INSPIRATIONAL COLORING BOOKS BY IRINA V. IVANOVA

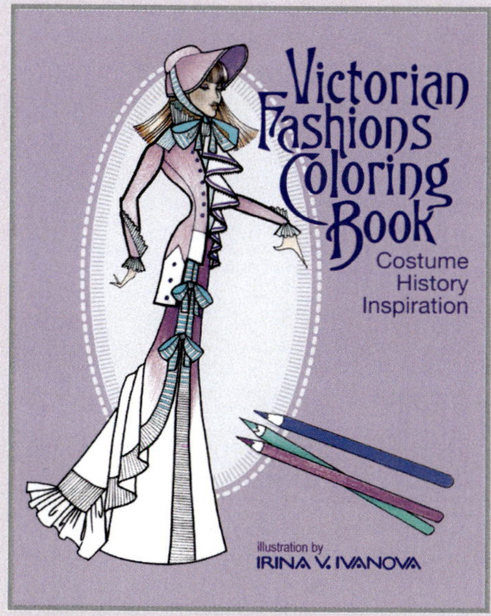


ISBN: 978-0984356010

ISBN: 979-8628735527

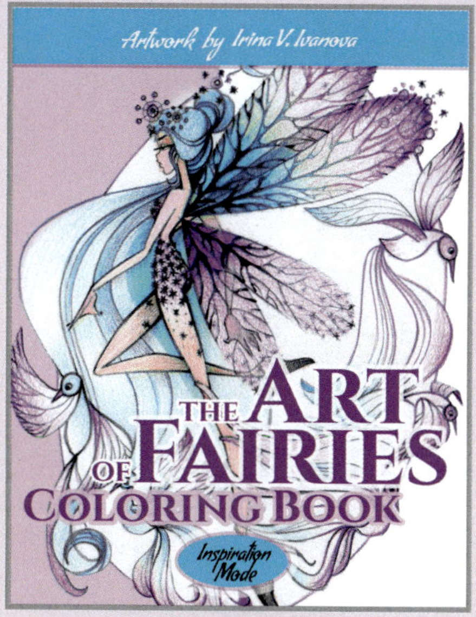


ISBN: 979-8631107472

ISBN: 978-1953408990

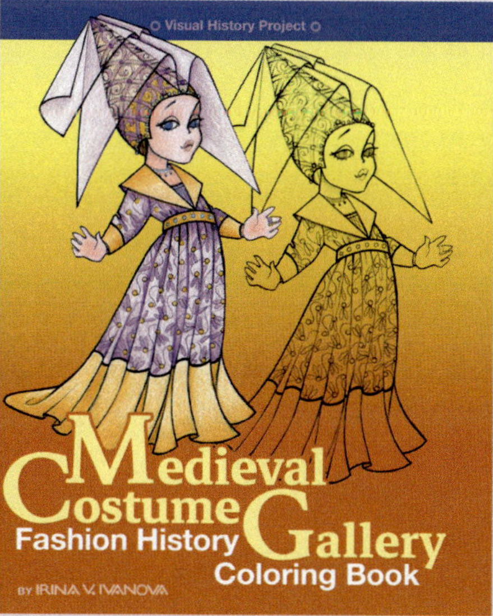


ISBN: 978-0984356089

ISBN: 978-0984356096

## FASHION DRAWING FOR FUTURE FASHION DESIGNERS

ISBN: 978-1953408105

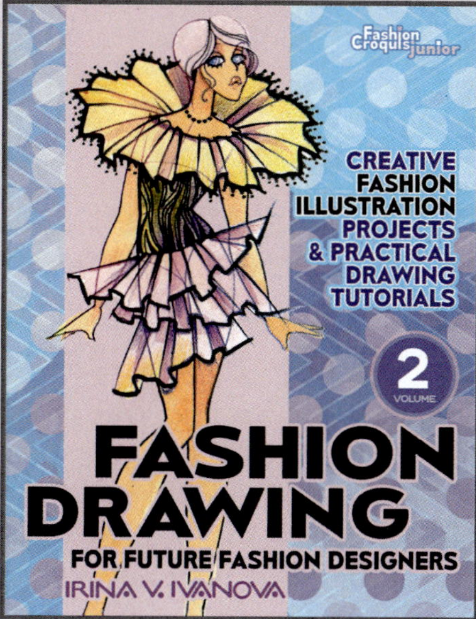


ISBN: 978-1953408112

ISBN: 978-1953408112

Made in the USA
Middletown, DE
29 March 2023